Sounds
and Music

Library Edition Published 1991

Published by Marshall Cavendish Corporation
2415 Jerusalem Avenue
PO Box 587, North Bellmore,
N.Y. 11710
Library edition produced by Pemberton Press

Printed in Italy by New Interlitho, Milan

© Marshall Cavendish Corporation 1991
© Cherrytree Press Ltd. 1990

Library of Congress Cataloging in-Publication Data

Kerrod, Robin
    Sounds and music / by Robin Kerrod : illustrated by Mike Atkinson,
        p. cm. – (Secrets of Science)
    Includes index.
    Summary: Projects, experiments, and activities explore the world
of sounds, both musical and otherwise.
        ISBN 1-85435-270-9
    1. Sound-waves – Juvenile literature. 2.. Sound-waves – Experiments –
Juvenile literature. 3. Music - Acoustics and physics Juvenile
literature. 4. Music –Acoustics and physics – Experiments – Juvenile
literature. (1. Sound – Experiments. 2. Music – Experiments.
3. Experimennts. 4. Scientific recreations.) I. Atkinson, Mike,
III. II. Title. iii. Series: Kerrod, Robin. Secrets of science.
QQC226.5,K39 1991
634 – dc20   80-25549
                                                                CIP
                                                                AC

SECRETS OF SCIENCE

Sounds and Music

Robin Kerrod

Illustrated by Mike Atkinson

MARSHALL CAVENDISH
NEW YORK · LONDON · TORONTO · SYDNEY

Safety First

☐ Ask your parents or another adult for permission before you start any experiment, especially if you are using matches or anything hot, sharp, or poisonous.

☐ Wear old clothes, or cover your clothes with an old shirt or apron.

☐ If you work on a table, use an old one and protect it with paper or cardboard.

☐ Do water experiments in the sink or outdoors.

☐ Strike matches away from your body, and make sure they are out before you thrown them away.

☐ Make sure candles are standing securely.

☐ Wear oven gloves when handling anything hot.

☐ Take care when cutting things. Always cut away from your body.

☐ Don't use cans with jagged edges. Use ones with lids.

☐ Use only non-toxic white glue, glue sticks, or paste.

☐ Never taste chemicals, unless the book tells you to.

☐ Label all bottles and jars containing chemicals, and store them where young children can't get at them—and not in the family food cupboard.

☐ Never use or play with household electricity. It can KILL. Use a flashlight or dry cell.

☐ When you have finished an experiment, put your things away, clean up, and wash your hands.

Contents

Good Vibrations

Listen. How many sounds can you hear? What sounds are they? Put your fingers in your ears. What can you hear now?

Sounds fill the air all around us. The air carries the sounds to our ears. If you twang a rubber band, you can see the band vibrating, or move up and down. Twang a ruler on a desk and you can see the same thing. What you cannot see is that the air next to the rubber band or ruler is moving, too.

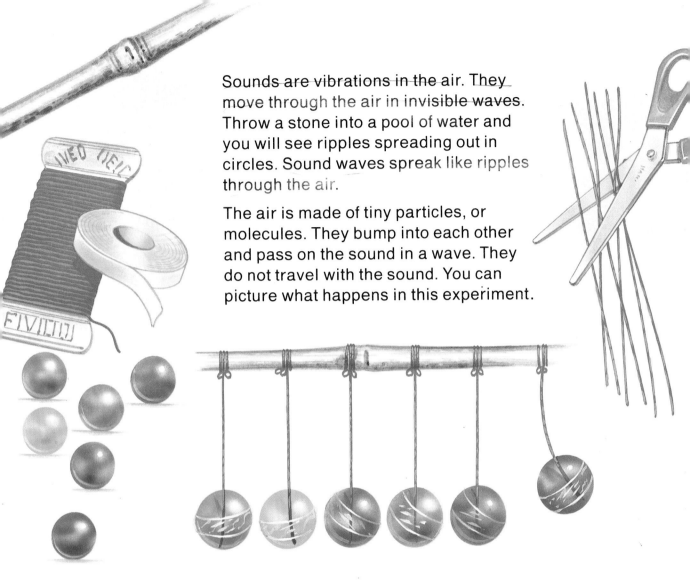

Sounds are vibrations in the air. They move through the air in invisible waves. Throw a stone into a pool of water and you will see ripples spreading out in circles. Sound waves spreak like ripples through the air.

The air is made of tiny particles, or molecules. They bump into each other and pass on the sound in a wave. They do not travel with the sound. You can picture what happens in this experiment.

To-ing and Fro-ing

1 You need a short stick or bamboo cane, string, some marbles, and tape.

2 Hang up the stick with two lengths of string.

3 Cut a length of string about 1 foot long for each marble. Tape one end to a marble and tie the other to the stick. Leave a small gap between the marbles.

4 Pull back the end marble and let go.

5 Each marble hits the next and passes on the motion. That last marble flies up. That is what happens to air particles.

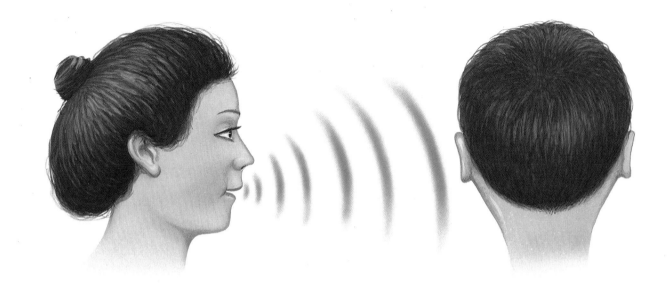

Voice and Hearing

Like all sounds, the sound of your voice is made by vibrations. Put your fingers on your throat and sing. Can you feel the vibrations?

In your throat, there are two little bands of tissue called vocal chords. When you speak, air passes up through your throat and makes the chords vibrate.

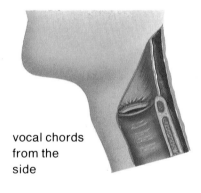

vocal chords from the side

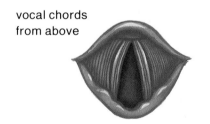

vocal chords from above

We hear sounds when sound waves reach our ears. The vibrations hit a thin disk of tissue called the eardrum. It vibrates like the surface of a real drum.

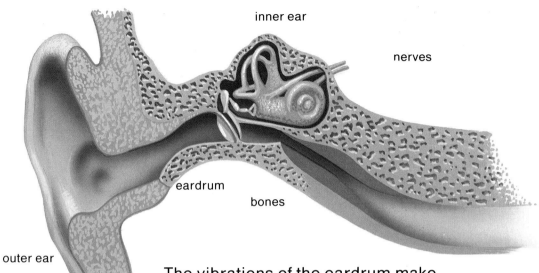

inner ear

nerves

eardrum

bones

outer ear

The vibrations of the eardrum make three little bones behind it vibrate. They pass the vibrations into the inner ear. There, the vibrations are turned into signals. Nerves carry the signals to the brain. When they reach the brain, we hear sounds.

Most large animals have ears and vocal chords like ours. They make all sorts of sounds. Cows moo, pigs grunt, sheep bleet, and so on. Insects have no vocal chords. The buzzing of bees is the sound of their wings beating.

Ear, Ear

Why do we need two ears? Wouldn't one do? Plug your ears with cotton. Get a friend to blindfold you, and place a ticking clock somewhere in the room. Turn around several times, then take out one earplug. Can you hear where the clock is? If you can't, take out the other plug. See what a difference two ears make. The brain needs two signals to work out where a sound comes from.

The part of the ear that we can see collects sounds and directs them into the ear. If we had larger ears, they would pick up more sound waves. Everything would sound louder.

Cup your hands behind your ears and hear the difference. Try using a plastic funnel like an old-fashioned ear trumpet.

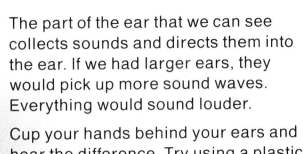

You can use a funnel to make a megaphone. This makes your voice sound louder. You speak through the small end. The sound waves cannot spread out so far, so they sound louder.

You can make a telephone using two funnels and a long piece of hose pipe. You only have to whisper to be heard.

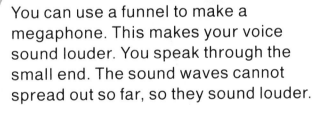

Traveling Sound

Sound waves travel through the air. Can they travel through other materials? Find out with this ticking clock experiment.

Put the clock at one end of a wooden table. Listen to its ticks. Cover one ear, and hold the other one against the tabletop. Can you still hear the ticking? Is it quieter or louder than the ticking through the air?

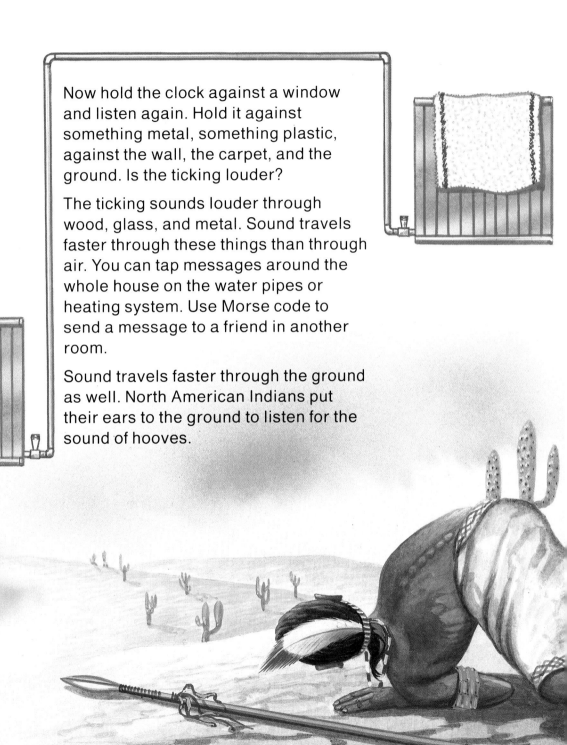

Now hold the clock against a window and listen again. Hold it against something metal, something plastic, against the wall, the carpet, and the ground. Is the ticking louder?

The ticking sounds louder through wood, glass, and metal. Sound travels faster through these things than through air. You can tap messages around the whole house on the water pipes or heating system. Use Morse code to send a message to a friend in another room.

Sound travels faster through the ground as well. North American Indians put their ears to the ground to listen for the sound of hooves.

Sound Fast and Slow

Sound travels well through water. If you put your head underwater, you can her yourself breathing. Don't try it unless you have an adult with you. It is very easy to drown.

Animals that live in the oceans send messages to each other by sound waves. Whales can ''talk'' to other whales a couple of miles away.

gas molecules

liquid molecules

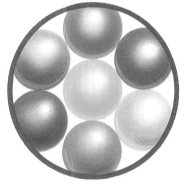

solid molecules

Sound travels through water and wood faster than through air because water and wood are denser than air.

Air is a gas. The molecules in a gas are far apart. Water is a liquid. The molecules in a liquid are closer together.

Wood is a solid. The molecules in a solid are even closer together. The closer the molecules are, the faster the sound is passed from one to the other.

The speed of sound is much lower than the speed of light. Thunder is the sound that lightning makes. But you do not often hear thunder at the moment you see a flash of lightning. If the storm is several miles away, you hear the thunder several seconds later.

String Calls

Even a piece of string carries sound better than air. Tie a piece of string to a fork and hit it with a spoon. Now, hold the string to your ear and hit the fork again. Does it sound louder?

You can make the sound even louder. Tie the fork to a metal pan and hold your ear close to the pan. Strike the fork again. The sound is amplified, which means that it is made louder. Microphones are instruments that amplify sound. They are used in telephones.

Make a String Telephone

1 You need two yogurt containers and a long length of string.

2 Get a friend to stand so far away from you that you cannot hear him or her speak. Make your piece of string about a yard longer than the distance between you.

3 Make a hole in one container, thread the string through it, and tie a knot inside.

4 Do the same with the other, and your telephone is ready for use. Stretch the string until it is taut and then speak. Can you and your friend hear each other now?

In the mouthpiece of a real telephone the sound of your voice makes a metal disk vibrate. The vibrations are changed into electrical waves that travel along the telephone wires. When these waves reach the earpiece of the other telephone, they make another disk vibrate. Its vibrations give off sound waves just like those that entered the telephone.

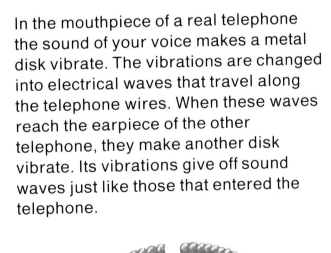

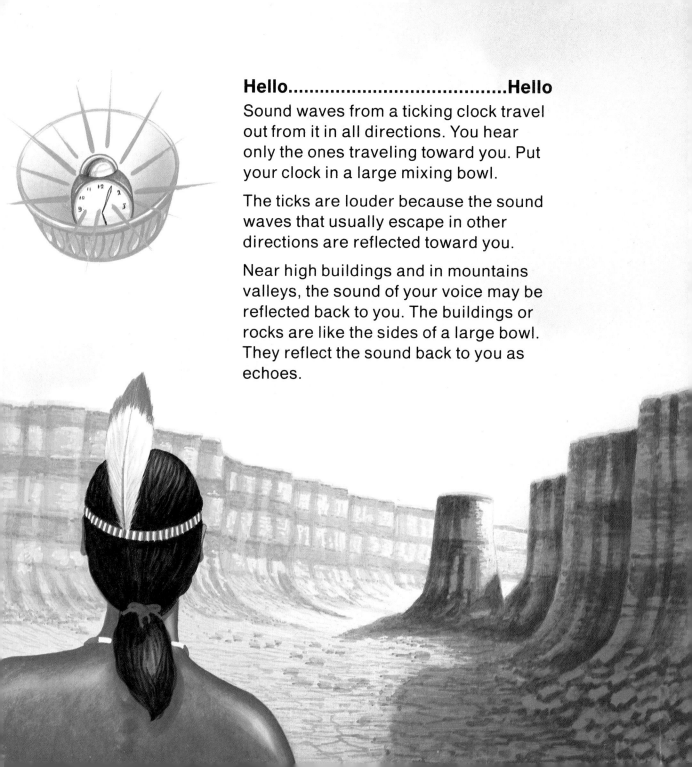

Hello...Hello

Sound waves from a ticking clock travel out from it in all directions. You hear only the ones traveling toward you. Put your clock in a large mixing bowl.

The ticks are louder because the sound waves that usually escape in other directions are reflected toward you.

Near high buildings and in mountains valleys, the sound of your voice may be reflected back to you. The buildings or rocks are like the sides of a large bowl. They reflect the sound back to you as echoes.

Bats use echoes to hunt for their food. They hunt in the dark by giving off bursts of sound. When the sound waves hit a tasty moth, the sounds are reflected back to the bat. Humans cannot hear the sounds the bats make. They are too high pitched for our ears. We call them ultrasounds.

Many boats use ultrasounds to find out where the seabed is, or where there are shoals of fish or wrecks. This method of finding things is called echolocation.

High and Low

Sounds can be nice or nasty, loud or soft, high or low. We call the highness or lowness of a sound its pitch. The pitch of a sound depends on how quickly the waves vibrate. The number of times a sound wave vibrates per second is called its frequency. The higher the frequency, the higher is the pitch.

Tuning Your Bicycle
1 You need a bicycle and a piece of thin plastic or cardboard, and something to fix it in position.

2 Fix the plastic so that it just touches the spokes of the bike with the wheel off the ground. Keep your fingers well away from the moving wheels.

3 Spin the wheel, and listen to the sound the plastic makes when it vibrates. The faster the wheel spins, the higher the pitch of the sound.

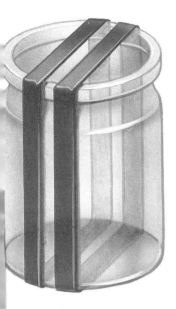

The pitch or frequency of a sound depends on the length of the wave. Stretch a rubber band over a jar and twang it. Now use a tighter band and twang it. Which makes the higher sound?

By making the band tighter, you made it shorter. The wave traveled a shorter distance, so there were more vibrations per second. The sound, or note, you produced was higher.

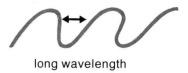

long wavelength

short wavelength

low frequency

high frequency

Blowing Bottles

1 You need a row of glass soft-drink bottles

2 Put increasing amounts of water in each bottle.

3 Blow across the tops of the bottles to make the air inside vibrate. Do the bottles with more water in them make higher or lower pitched sounds?

Nasty Noise and Sweet Music

Not all sounds are pleasant. We call sounds that we do not like noise. Most people dislike clattering, banging, throbbing, grating, or whining sounds. They hate the sound of road drills, alarms, and badly played music.

All these things give off irregular (not smooth) patterns of sound waves which jar on our ears. Their noise irritates us and makes us feel tired.

Loud or intense noise can damage our ears and make us deaf. People who use road drills or work with loud machinery wear earmuffs to protect their ears.

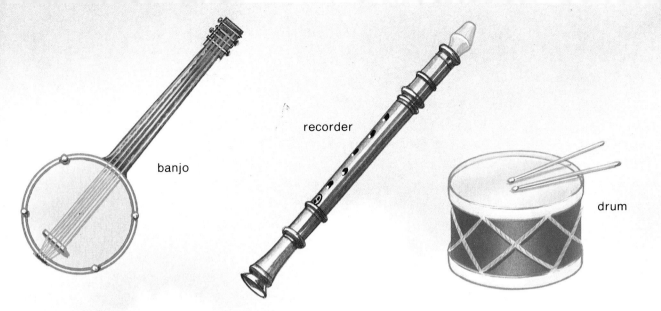

banjo

recorder

drum

Most of us like the sound of music. Music is sound that has regular (smooth) patterns of waves. Music is made by instruments that send out vibrations.

There are three main types of musical instruments. Stringed instruments have strings which you pluck or scrape to make them vibrate. Wind instruments are tubes that you blow through to make air vibrate. You hit percussion instruments to make them vibrate.

Sweet Whine
You can make your own musical instrument with a wine glass. Partly fill the glass with water. Then, wet your finger and rub it smoothly round the rim of the glass. What kind of sound does it make?

23

String Sounds

A rubber band stretched over a jar makes a louder sound than a rubber band on its own. When the band vibrates, it makes the air in the jar vibrate. The jar is amplifying the sound. Most stringed instruments amplify their sounds. Guitars and violins have strings stretched across a hollow wooden box.

A zither is a stringed instrument that is plucked. Authentic zithers have as many as forty strings. You can make a simple one with two rubber bands.

violin

guitar

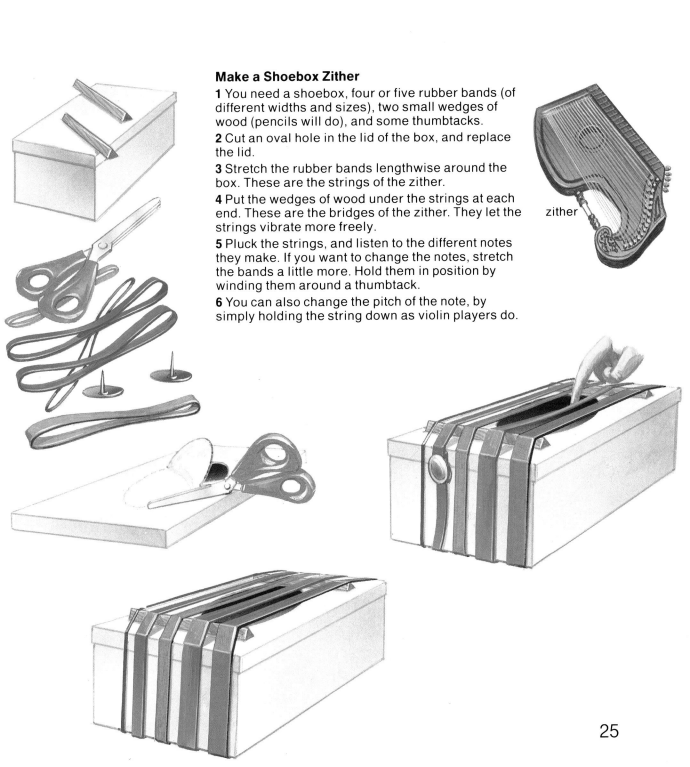

Make a Shoebox Zither

1 You need a shoebox, four or five rubber bands (of different widths and sizes), two small wedges of wood (pencils will do), and some thumbtacks.

2 Cut an oval hole in the lid of the box, and replace the lid.

3 Stretch the rubber bands lengthwise around the box. These are the strings of the zither.

4 Put the wedges of wood under the strings at each end. These are the bridges of the zither. They let the strings vibrate more freely.

5 Pluck the strings, and listen to the different notes they make. If you want to change the notes, stretch the bands a little more. Hold them in position by winding them around a thumbtack.

6 You can also change the pitch of the note, by simply holding the string down as violin players do.

zither

25

Alpine horn

flute

Playing the Pipes

If you blow over the top of an empty bottle, it gives you a musical note. This is because you have made the air inside vibrate. If you put some water in the bottle, the note will change. The "column" of air will have become shorter, and the note will be higher.

Some musical instruments make sounds by making a column of air vibrate. They are called wind instruments.

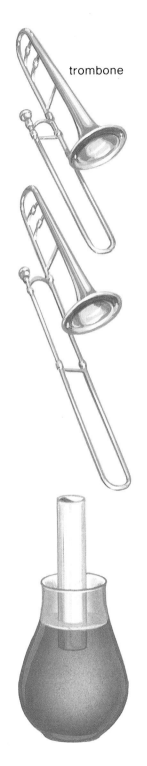

trombone

Some wind instruments are made of brass; some are made of wood. You change the notes played by different instruments in different ways. The recorder and flute have holes in the pipe. The player covers the holes or leaves them open. To play the bugle, you change the amount of air you blow through the pipe with your lips

French horn

Make a Trombone in a Bottle

1 You need a bottle or vase and a plastic or cardboard tube that can move freely in and out of the bottle. You can use a drinking straw.

2 Fill the bottle almost to the top with water, and lower the tube into it. Blow across the top of the tube and listen to the note.

3 Push the tube farther into the water. Now you have made the column of air in the tube shorter. Blow over the top again. Is the note lower or higher?

Playing Your Bicycle Pump

You can use your bicycle pump to make music in the same way. Blow over the open end while moving the handle in and out.

27

cymbals

triangle

Crashing and Banging

Everything gives out some sort of sound when you strike it. Musical instruments that work by striking are called percussion instruments. They include drums and chimes, cymbals, and triangles.

A drum has a skin stretched across a hollow frame. When you hit the drum, the skin vibrates and makes the air inside vibrate. If the skin is tight or small, the drum sounds a high note. If the drum is small inside, it holds only a small amount of air, so the note is high. Bigger drums sound lower notes.

drum

timpanum

Make a Drum

1 You need a mixing bowl, a sheet of strong plastic, and some tape.

2 Stretch the plastic tautly over the bowl, and tape it around the side so that it is airtight.

3 Play the drum by tapping it with your fingers or with sticks.

4 If you use different size bowls, you can make several drums and listen to the different notes they make.

Make a Lot of Noise

1 Make some chimes out of lengths of metal piping. Hang them up, and hit them with a long nail. Each size gives out a different note.

2 Make a xylophone with a set of wine glasses. Leave one empty and fill the rest with increasing amounts of water. This will give you different notes when you strike them. Hit them gently with a teaspoon.

3 Use a pair of flat saucepan lids to make cymbals.

4 For a finger-tapping rhythm to accompany the music, fit thimbles on your fingers. Use them to ''play'' a metal tray.

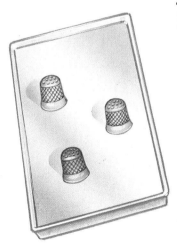

The Power of Sound

Sound is very powerful. It can make people deaf, and it can give them a shock. If you blow up a paper bag and hold the neck tight so that air cannot escape, you can make a really loud sound. Simply smash the bag with your hands. As the bag splits, the air rushes out with a bang. Never try this trick when people are not expecting it. It can be dangerous.

The air rushes out of the bag with a great force. It makes a high-pressure wave, called a shock wave.

Engineers use shock waves to knock down buildings. They set off explosives that send out shock waves powerful enough to make the building collapse. The explosives do not actually come into contact with the building.

One Last Note!

Please remember that what you think of as music may be just noise to somebody else. Do stop "playing" if you find that the noise you are making is annoying those around you.

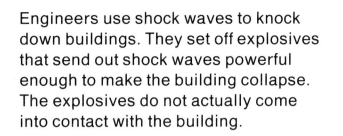

Index and glossary